really easy piano

MOVIE
MUSICALS

ISBN: 978-1-5400-6668-8

Visit Hal Leonard Online at
www.halleonard.com

Contact us:
Hal Leonard
7777 West Bluemound Road
Milwaukee, WI 53213
Email: info@halleonard.com

In Europe, contact:
Hal Leonard Europe Limited
42 Wigmore Street
Marylebone, London, W1U 2RY
Email: info@halleonardeurope.com

In Australia, contact:
Hal Leonard Australia Pty. Ltd.
4 Lentara Court
Cheltenham, Victoria, 3192 Australia
Email: info@halleonard.com.au

MOVIE MUSICALS

really easy piano

Always Remember Us This Way

from A Star Is Born

Words and Music by Stefani Germanotta, Hillary Lindsey, Natalie Hemby and Lori McKenna

This country-style song was written by Lady Gaga for the 2018 film, *A Star Is Born*, along with Natalie Hemby, Lori McKenna and Hillary Lindsey, who've worked with country artists such as Little Big Town and Carrie Underwood. To date, there are four versions of this iconic film, with Lady Gaga and Bradley Cooper starring in the most recent release and the first dating back to 1937!

Hints & Tips: Choose a very steady tempo for this one; there are some tricky rhythms and a lot of sixteenth notes. Have a listen to the song first.

Moderately slow ballad ♩ = 60

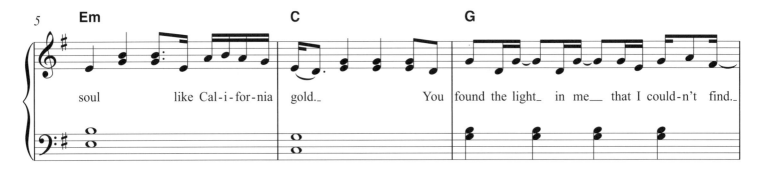

Beauty and the Beast
from Beauty and the Beast

Music by Alan Menken
Lyrics by Howard Ashman

The 1991 classic movie was among the first Disney cartoons to undergo a live action remake,
which was released in 2017 and starred Emma Watson as Belle. The accompanying song of the same title
was originally a duet sung by Celine Dion and Peabo Bryson, who handed over the reins to
pop princess Ariana Grande and soul man John Legend for the 2017 film.

Hints & Tips: Make sure the eighth notes are rhythmical throughout. Think carefully about
the note your right-hand thumb needs to be on — it's not the same all the way through.

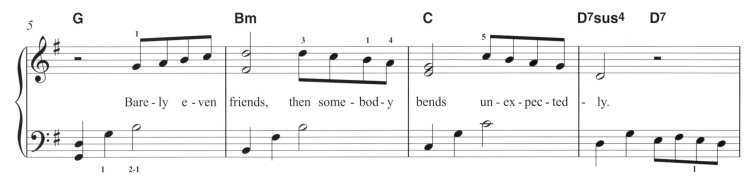

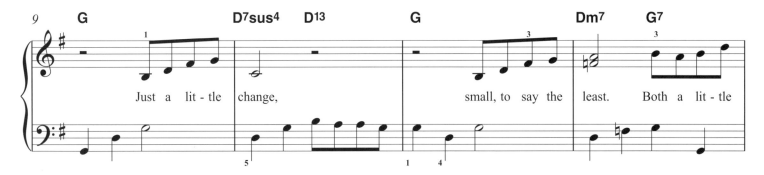

Bohemian Rhapsody
from Bohemian Rhapsody

Words and Music by Freddie Mercury

Through a fusion of the late Freddie Mercury's master recordings, Canadian singer Marc Martel and lead actor Rami Malek's vocals, the 2018 film *Bohemian Rhapsody* resurrected the legendary Queen frontman's voice for audiences worldwide. The film was widely acclaimed, particularly with reference to Malek's haunting portrayal of Freddie Mercury. *Bohemian Rhapsody* won numerous awards, most notably four Oscars that included Best Actor for Malek.

Hints & Tips: Bring out the harmonies at the start as they play a big part in the feel of the song.
Play through the passages with accidentals thoroughly as some of these are quite tricky.

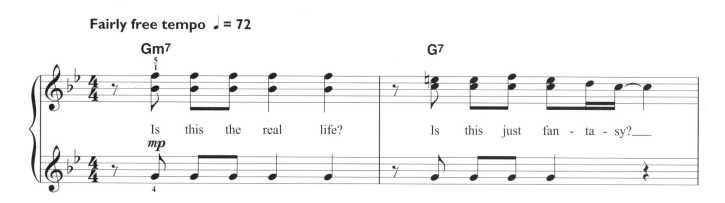

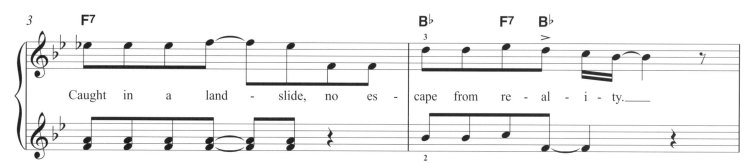

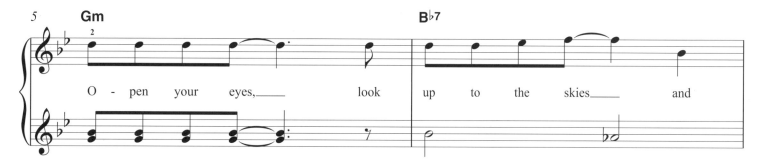

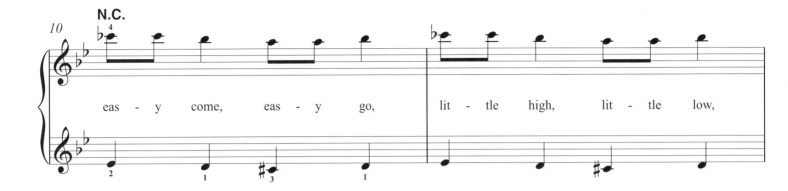

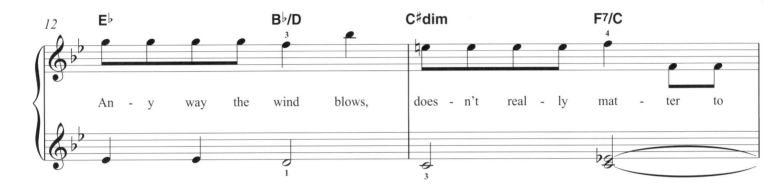

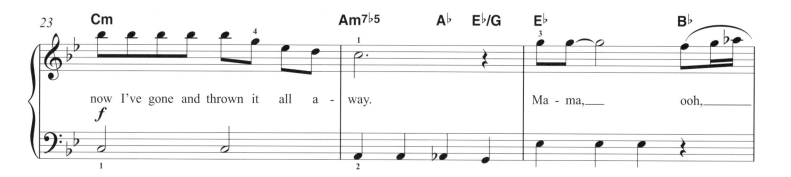

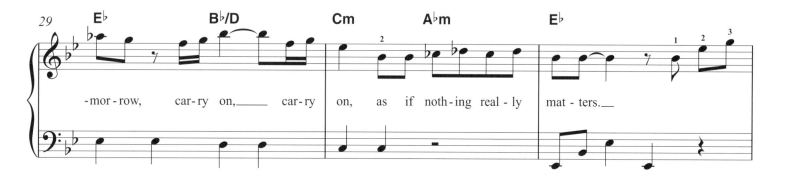

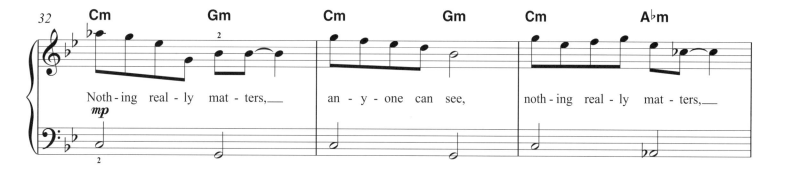

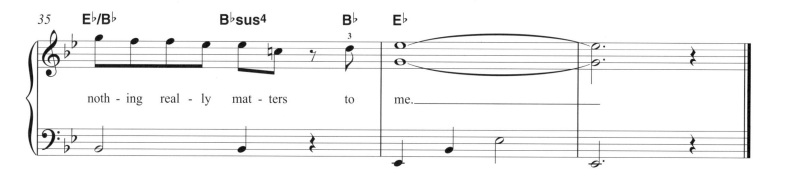

City of Stars
from La La Land

Music by Justin Hurwitz
Lyrics by Benj Pasek & Justin Paul

Emma Stone and Ryan Gosling star as Mia and Sebastian in the movie *La La Land*, released in 2016 and directed by Damien Chazelle. This duet between the two was performed live on set and requested by Gosling to be in a particularly low key for his voice, to suit his character. Composed by Justin Hurwitz, with help from Benj Pasek and Justin Paul, this song won the Oscar for Best Original Song 2017, while Hurwitz himself won the Oscar for Best Score in the same year.

Hints & Tips: Practice the arpeggio figure in each hand separately first, taking care to get the swing rhythm.
The song should sound free and easy, although the pulse becomes more insistent at the bottom of the second page.

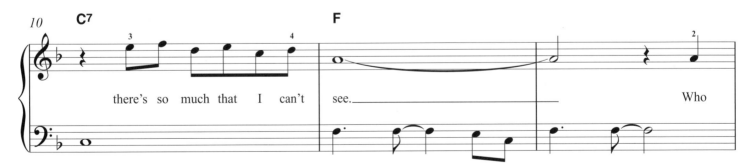

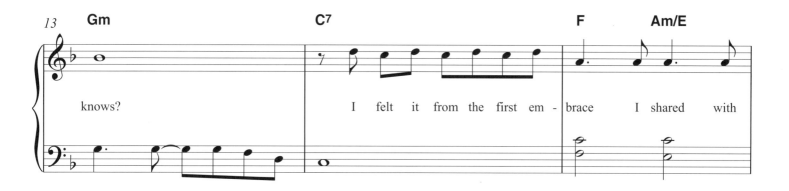

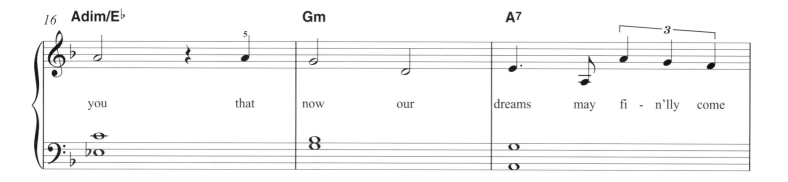

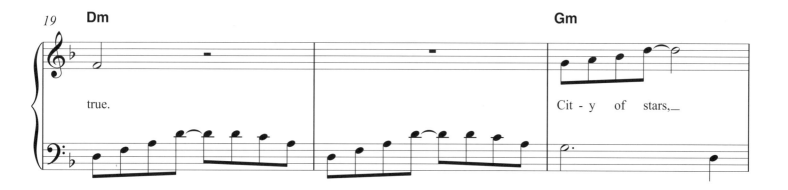

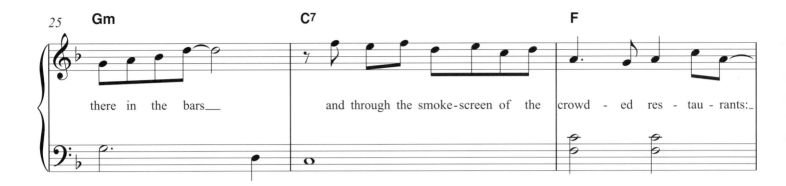

there in the bars___ and through the smoke-screen of the crowd - ed res - tau - rants:_

___ it's love. Yes, all we're look - ing for is

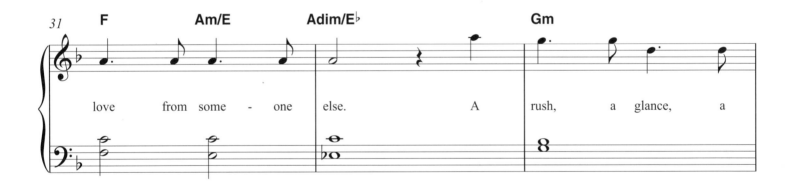

love from some - one else. A rush, a glance, a

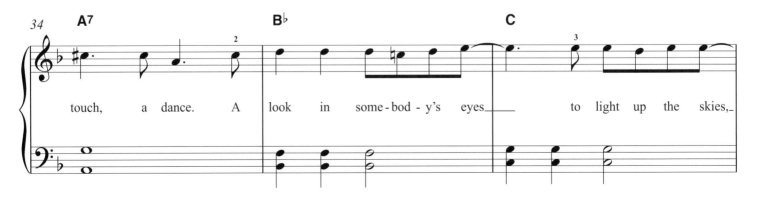

touch, a dance. A look in some-bod - y's eyes___ to light up the skies,_

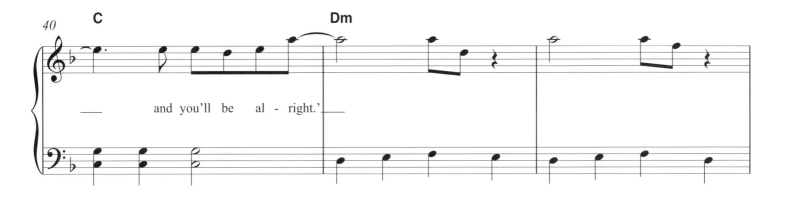

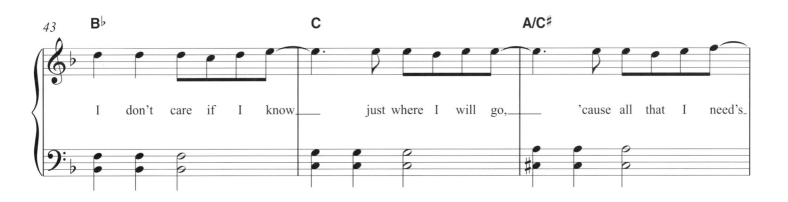

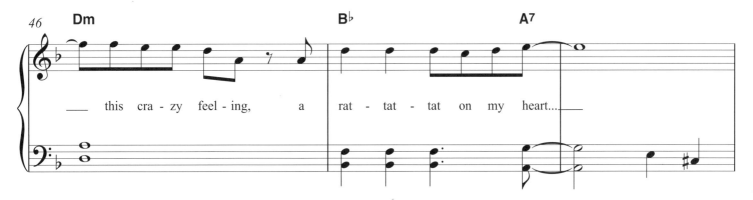

Think I want it to stay.

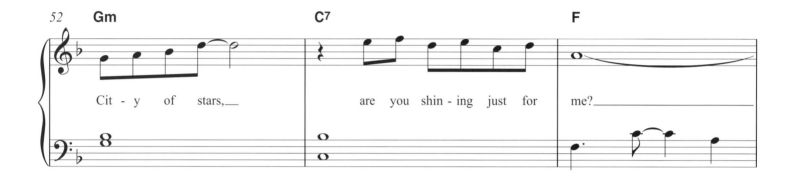

City of stars,_____ are you shin - ing just for me?_____

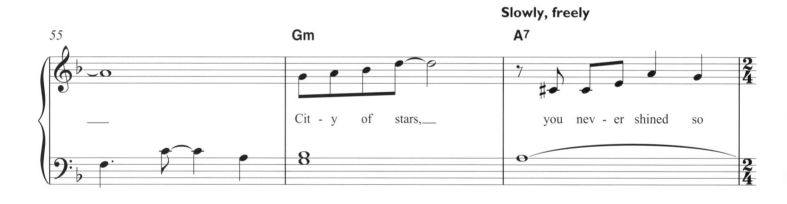

_____ City of stars,_____ you nev - er shined so

bright - ly._____

Fernando
from Mamma Mia! Here We Go Again

Words and Music by Benny Andersson, Bjorn Ulvaeus and Stig Anderson

'Fernando', originally going by the working title of 'Tango', was first recorded in Swedish by Anni-Frid 'Frida' Lyngstad on a solo record before it appeared on ABBA's *Greatest Hits* album in 1975. The song reached No. 1 in an impressive thirteen countries, including the UK, Australia and Mexico. It appears on the soundtrack for the second *Mamma Mia!* film, *Mamma Mia! Here We Go Again*, released in 2018 and starring Amanda Seyfriend and Lily James.

Hints & Tips: This is a good one for practicing thirds and sixths in the right hand. Don't worry too much about the fingering when playing the sixths, and leave out the bottom note if it's a problem.

you were hum - ming to your - self and soft - ly strum - ming your gui -

C

- tar.   I could hear the dis - tant drums and sounds of bu - gle calls were com - ing from a -

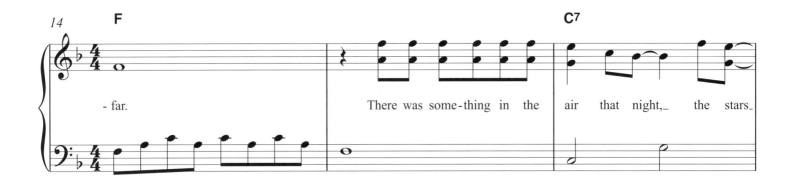

F   **C7**

- far.   There was some - thing in the air that night,_ the stars_

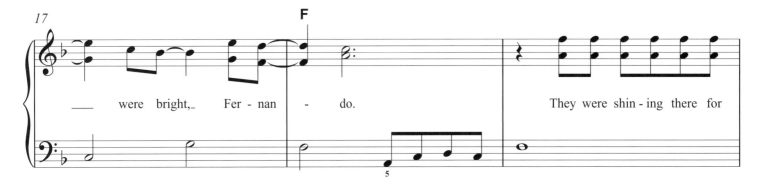

                                                                    F

___ were bright,_ Fer - nan - do.   They were shin - ing there for

5

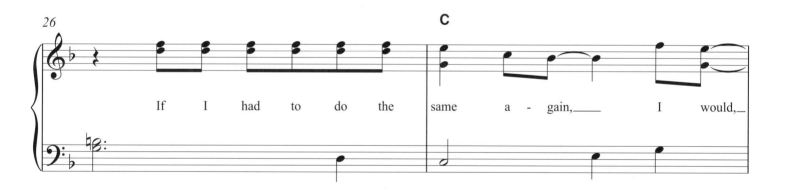

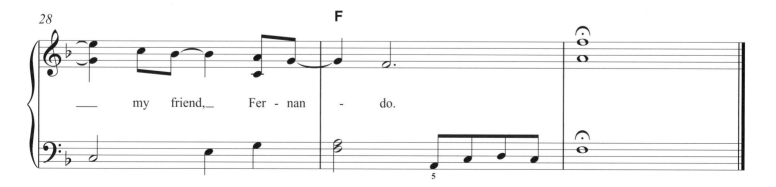

I Dreamed a Dream

from Les Misérables

Music by Claude-Michel Schönberg
Lyrics by Alain Boublil, Jean-Marc Natel and Herbert Kretzmer

This heartbreaking song, sung by the tragic character Fantine in *Les Misérables*, chronicles her summer love with a rich student, with whom she fell pregnant before he abandoned her to bring up daughter Cosette alone. Anne Hathaway tackled the moving ballad in the 2012 film adaptation and was hailed for her role as Fantine. Hathaway was so dedicated to the character that they used her real hair in the scene where Fantine has it cut off!

Hints & Tips: Play around with the rhythm in the right hand, eg. feel free to add dotted rhythms here and there. Just make sure to keep the left hand firmly on the beat.

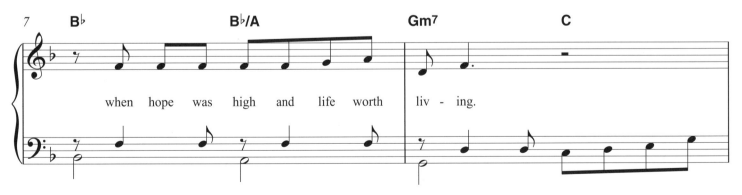

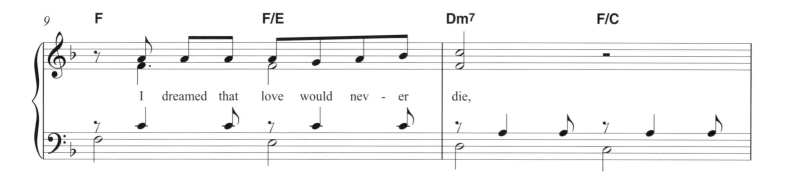

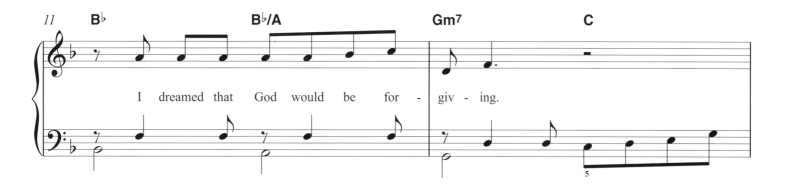

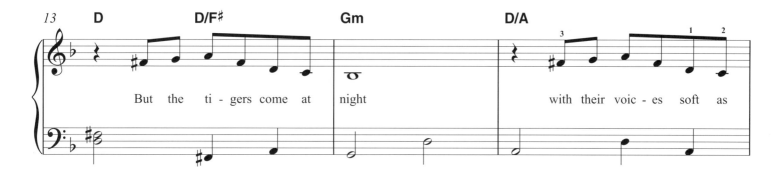

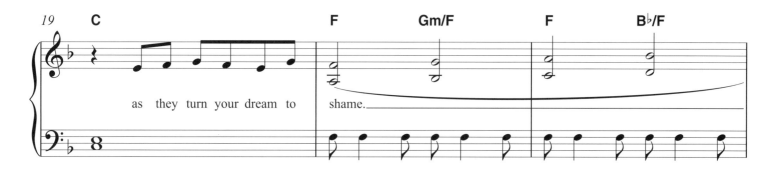

And still I dreamed he'd come to me,

that we would live the years to - geth - er. But there are dreams that can - not

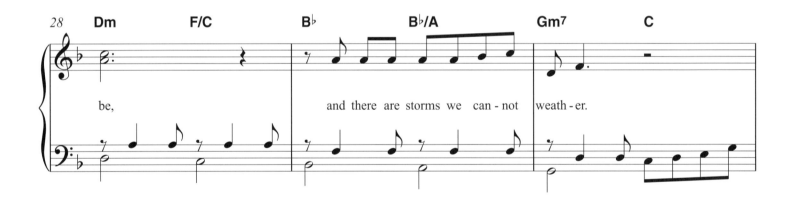

be, and there are storms we can - not weath - er.

I had a dream my life would

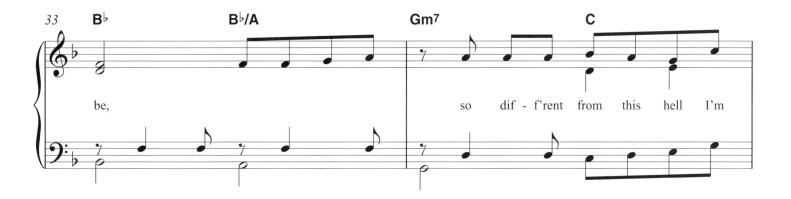

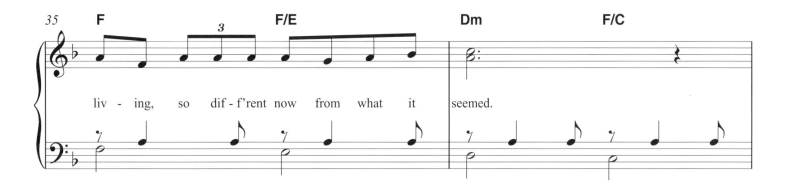

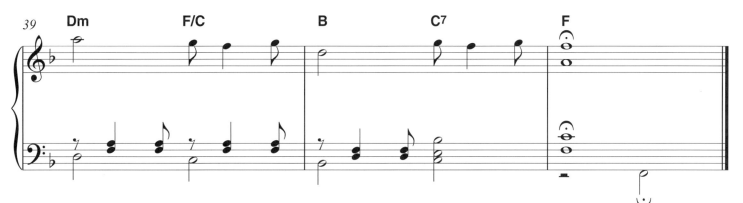

Mamma Mia
from Mamma Mia! Here We Go Again

Words and Music by Benny Andersson, Bjorn Ulvaeus and Stig Anderson

This was a no. 1 hit for ABBA in 1976, which inspired the long-running musical of the same name that opened in 2001, followed by two *Mamma Mia!* movies — the first released in 2008 and *Mamma Mia! Here We Go Again* in 2018. The song appears in the scene where a young Donna, Tanya and Rosie are rehearsing their act, Donna & The Dynamos. All three actors have backgrounds in music and recorded their own vocals for the film.

Hints & Tips: Keep the left-hand accompaniment light and place an emphasis on the first quarter note of each bar to avoid it sounding monotonous. This will also give the arrangement a stronger sense of pulse.

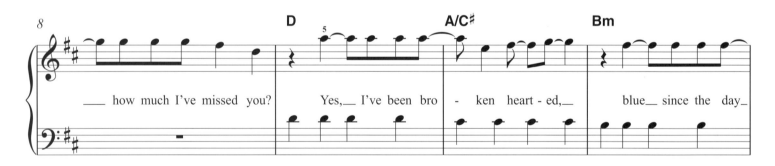

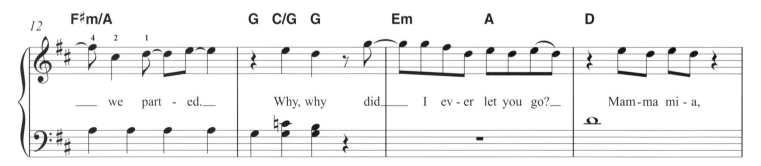

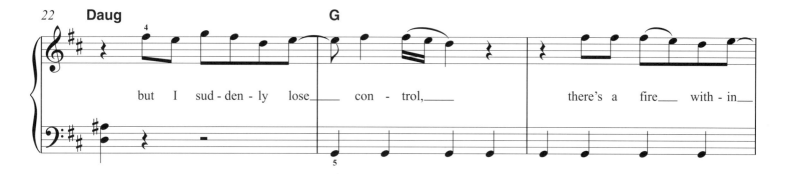

A Million Dreams
from The Greatest Showman

Words and Music by Benj Pasek and Justin Paul

Writing duo Benj Pasek and Justin Paul penned this tune for the 2017 film *The Greatest Showman*. In the movie, it is sung by a young P.T. Barnum (played by Ziv Zaifman), followed by the adult Barnum (Hugh Jackman) in a duet with his wife (Michelle Williams). The song gives the audience insight into Barnum's vision for his life, with Justin Paul explaining that 'he still has that dream and he still hasn't found that thing. So that dream is kept alive.'

Hints & Tips: In several places the melody line passes from the right hand to the left hand, and back again, eg. bar 8. Try and bring this out. When you get to the chorus, practice the right-hand part on its own at first to get the hang of the off-beat rhythm.

Moderately, with intensity ♩ = 74

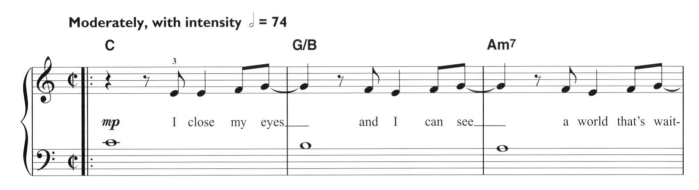

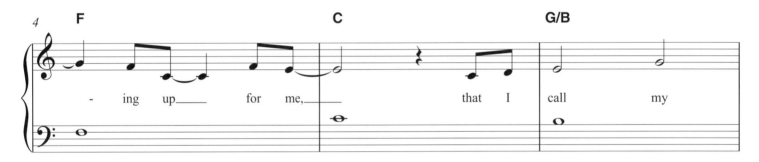

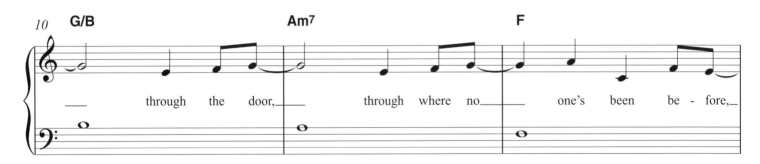

but it feels like home.

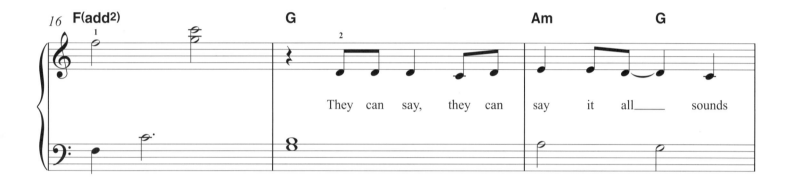

They can say, they can say it all___ sounds

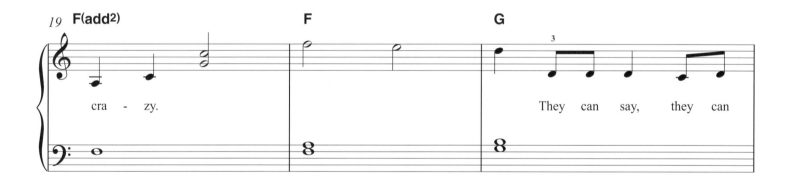

cra - zy.   They can say, they can

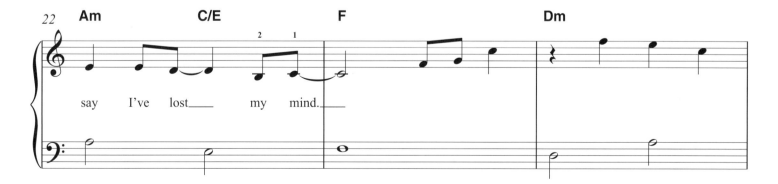

say I've lost___ my mind.___

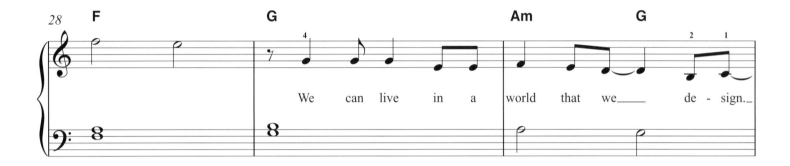

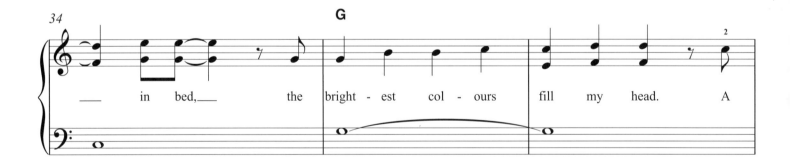

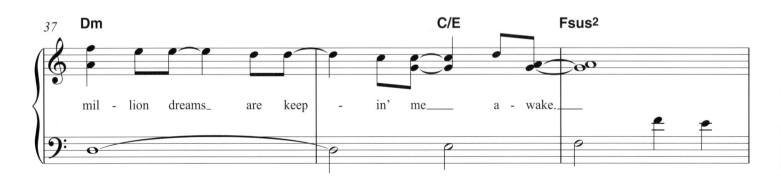

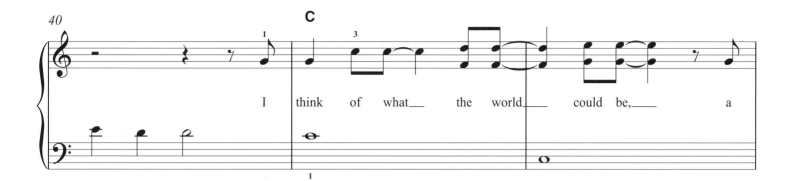

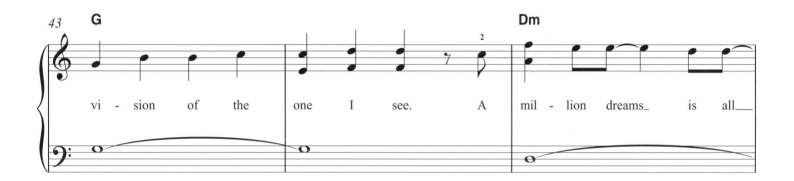

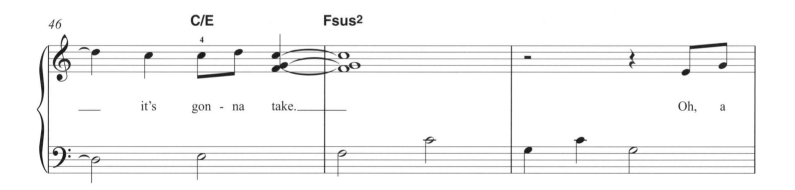

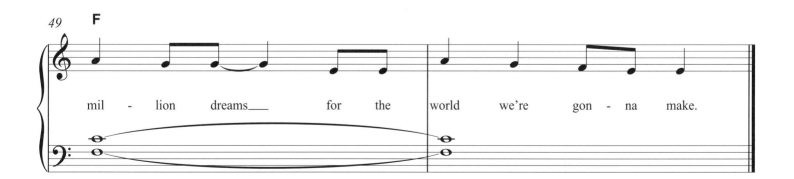

Radio Ga Ga
from Bohemian Rhapsody

Words and Music by Roger Taylor

Radio Ga Ga was included in the recreation of Queen's Live Aid performance at the end of the 2018 film, *Bohemian Rhapsody*. Rami Malek, who plays Freddie Mercury, worked tirelessly to replicate the frontman's performance, widely considered to be Queen's greatest live appearance. Videos have surfaced online comparing Malek's interpretation with the real footage of the band in 1985, which shows his commitment to mirroring Mercury's energy and movements throughout the set.

Hints & Tips: Keep the beat strong and steady in this one and be wary of accidentals.

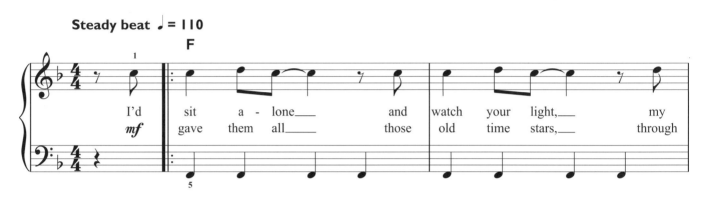

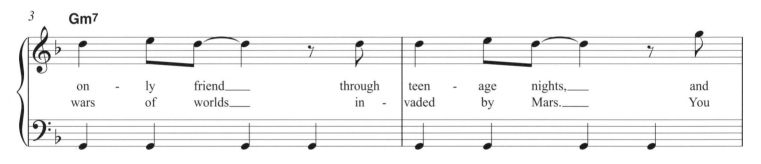

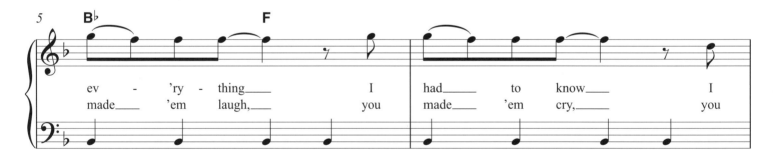

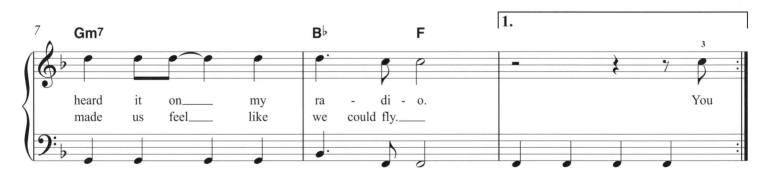

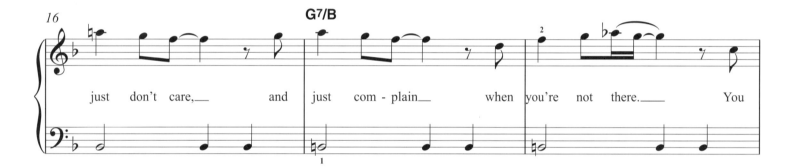

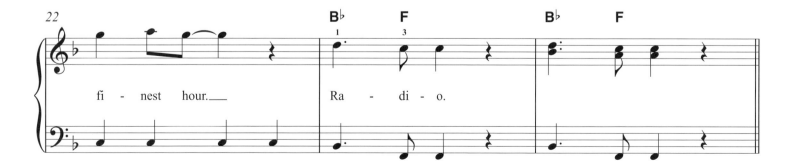

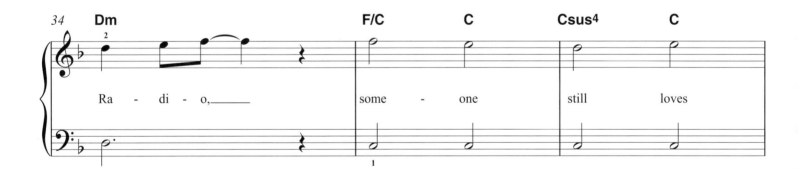

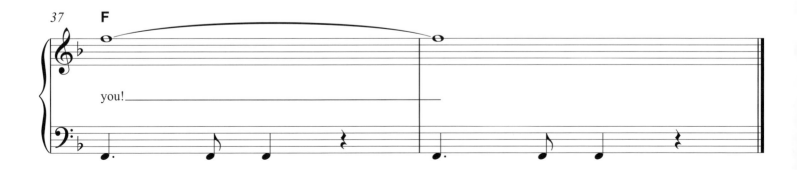

Rocket Man
(I Think It's Gonna Be A Long Long Time)
from Rocketman

Words and Music by Elton John and Bernie Taupin

Taron Egerton played Elton John in the 2019 film, *Rocketman*, to the delight of the public, film critics and even Elton himself. The title track of the film appears in a scene where Elton throws himself into a swimming pool and discovers his younger self singing the song on the pool floor. Egerton performed his own vocals for the film, with coaching from Elton, and the pair have performed live together a number of times since the film's release.

Hints & Tips: This song has a complex and varied vocal line. The right hand imitates this, and if you find the rhythm tricky, try marking in the beats of each bar with a pencil. This should help you to fit the sixteenth note rhythms with the left-hand part. The left hand stays quite still, so practice this first until it is secure.

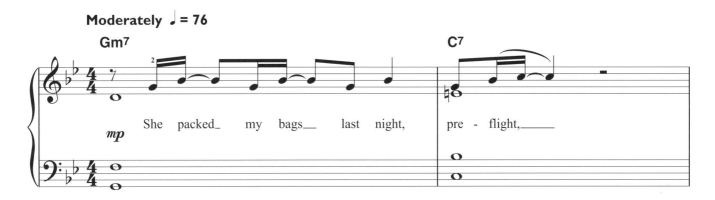

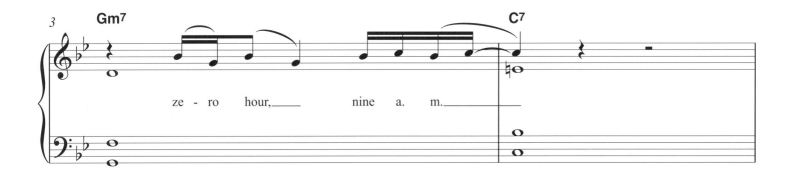

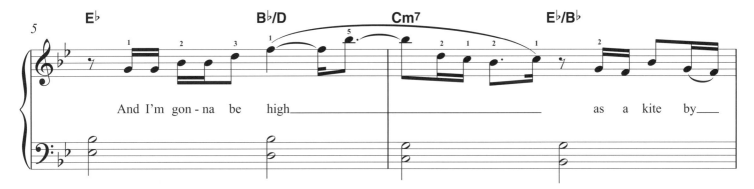

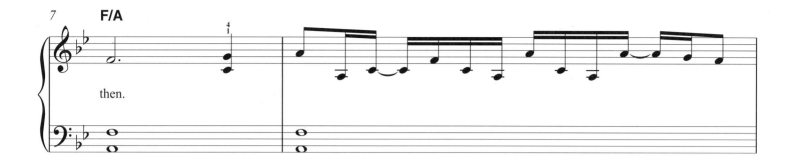

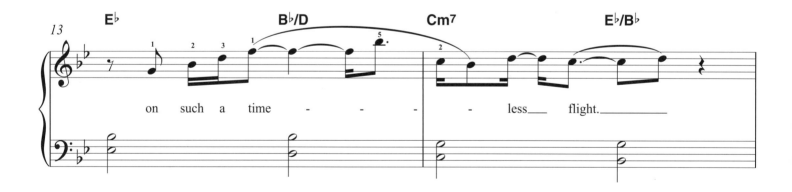

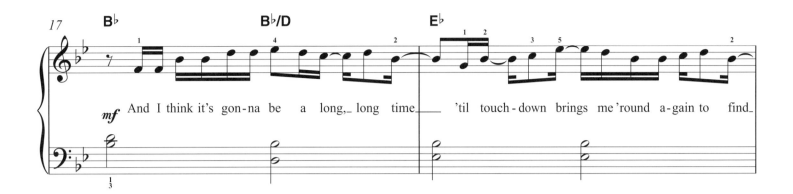

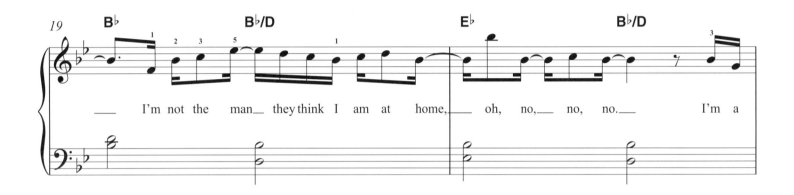

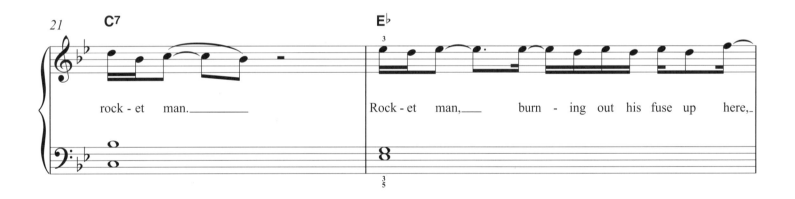

Speechless
from Aladdin

Music by Alan Menken
Lyrics by Benj Pasek and Justin Paul

Sung by Naomi Scott, who plays Jasmine in the 2019 *Aladdin* movie, this song sends a powerful message about having a voice and speaking up against injustice. It was an addition to the original 1992 soundtrack by Alan Menken, Tim Rice and Howard Ashman. As Menken says, 'it was obvious that Jasmine needed to move from being a Disney animated princess to a three-dimensional young woman who wants to be heard and respected.'

Hints & Tips: Be careful not to start too fast, or else the right-hand eighth notes will feel too busy. There are some wide intervals in the left hand, eg. bar 14. Don't let your wrist sag.

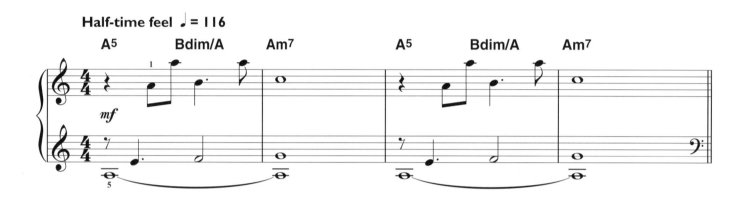

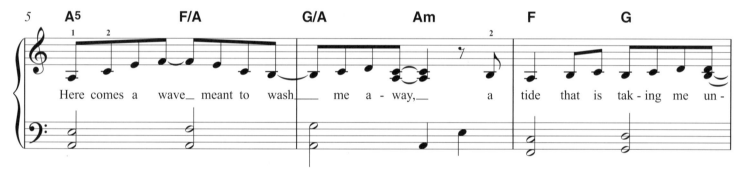

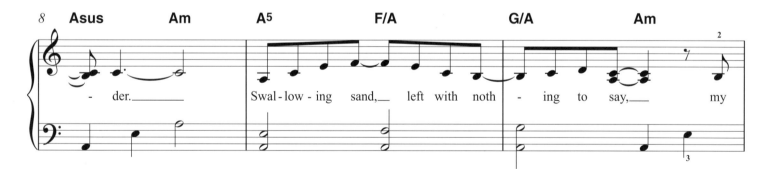

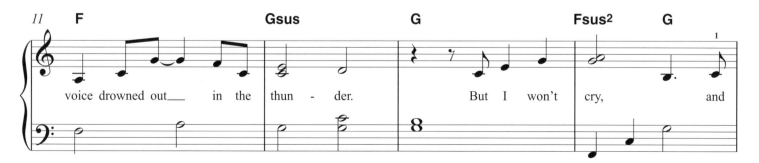

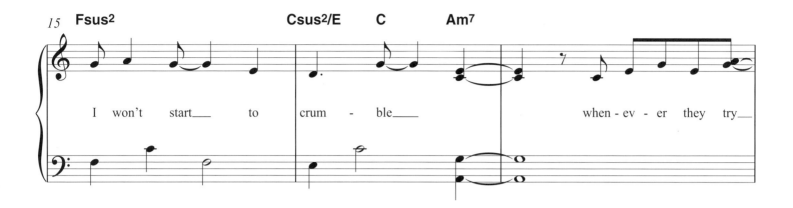

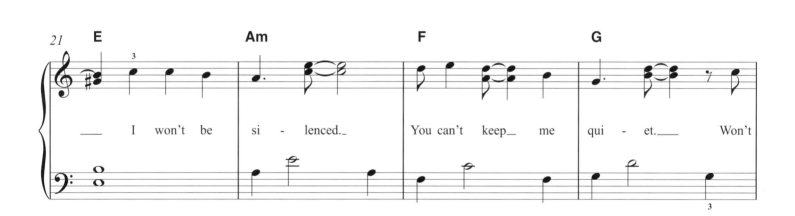

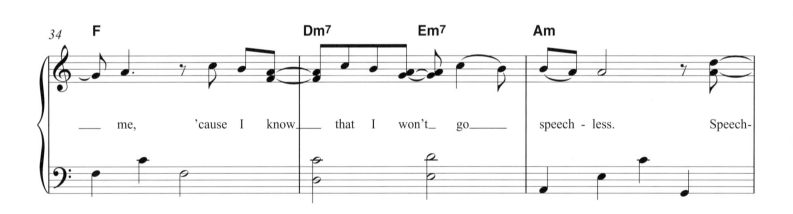

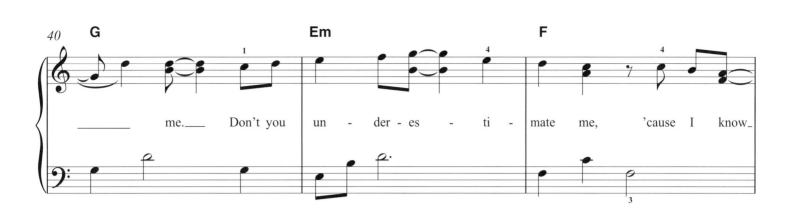

me.____ Don't you un - der - es - ti - mate me, 'cause I know____

____ that I won't__ go____ speech - less. All I know____ is I won't__ go speech-

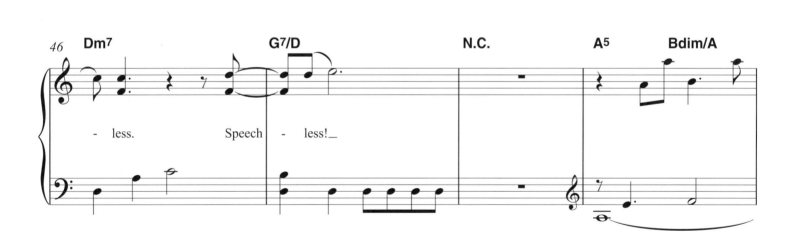

- less. Speech - less!__

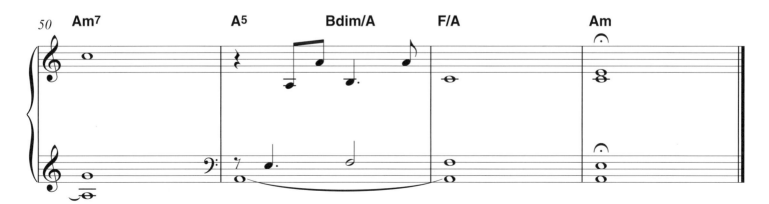

Suddenly
from Les Misérables

Music by Claude-Michel Schönberg
Lyrics by Herbert Kretzmer and Alain Boublil

This song marks a turning point for one of *Les Misérables'* main characters, Jean Valjean, when he experiences love for the first time in his life. It's a particularly poignant tune because the love he speaks of is for the young Cosette whom he adopts and raises as his own. In the film adaptation of the stage musical, released in 2012, Valjean is played by Hugh Jackman and the young Cosette by Isabelle Allen.

Hints & Tips: Practice hands separately first. There are several places where the right hand has large intervals to negotiate, eg. bar 9. If you struggle to reach both notes, just leave out the lower one. The same goes for the bottom of the second page.

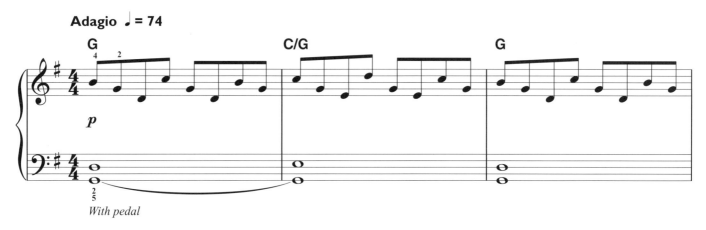

Sud - den - ly you're here, sud - den - ly it starts.

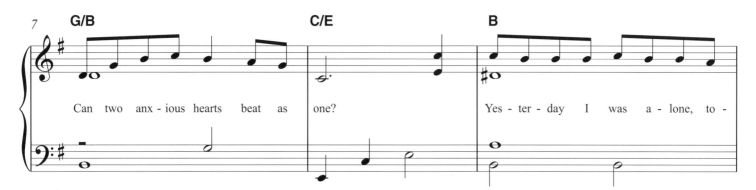

Can two anx - ious hearts beat as one? Yes - ter - day I was a - lone, to-

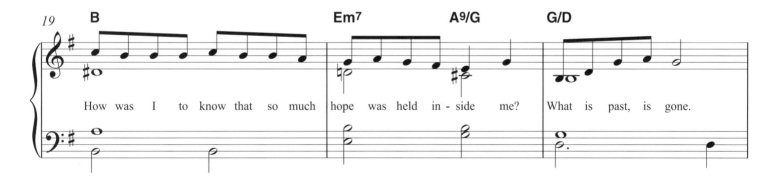

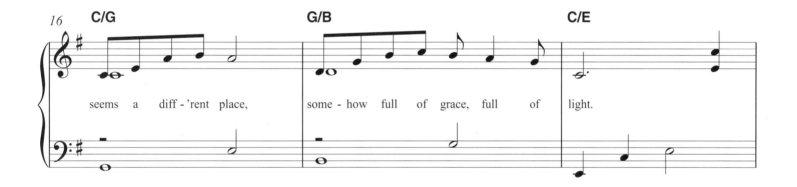

poco accel.   a little faster

41

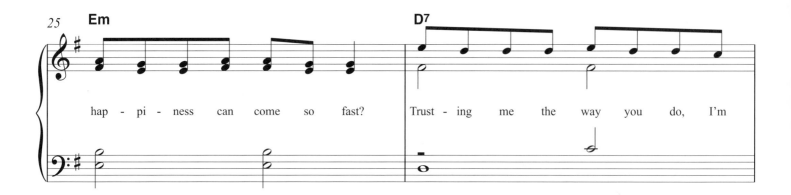

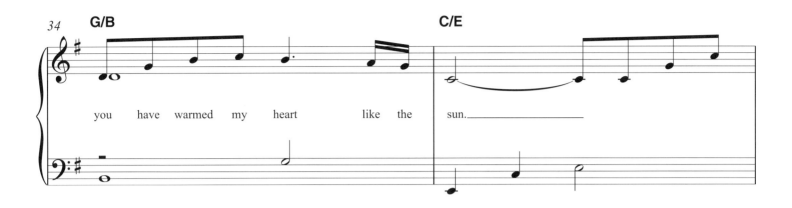

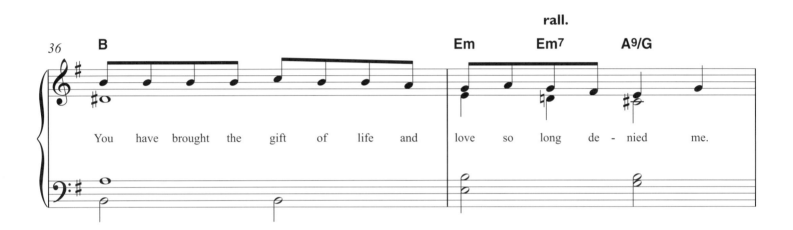

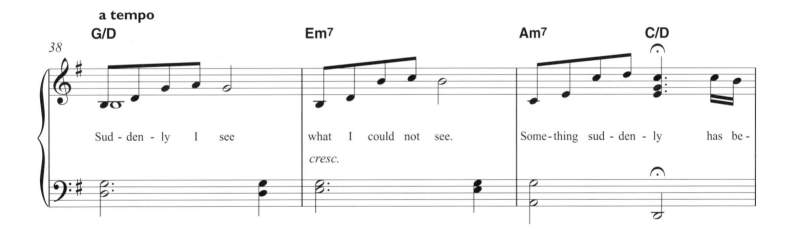

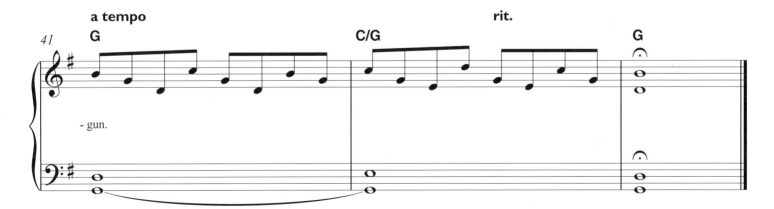

Shallow
from A Star Is Born

Words and Music by Stefani Germanotta, Mark Ronson, Andrew Wyatt and Anthony Rossomando

The most popular song to come out of the 2018 film *A Star Is Born*, 'Shallow' is sung by Lady Gaga and Bradley Cooper, who play lovers Ally and Jackson in the film. It won the Golden Globe for Best Original Song from a Motion Picture and the Oscar for Best Original Song, both in 2019. Gaga says of the film, 'I'm so proud to be part of a movie that addresses mental health issues. They're so important and a lot of artists deal with that.'

Hints & Tips: Practice the right hand on its own first, to get the hang of the syncopated (off-beat) rhythm. Sometimes the left hand joins in with this rhythm, other times it is on the beat. Keep a steady pulse.

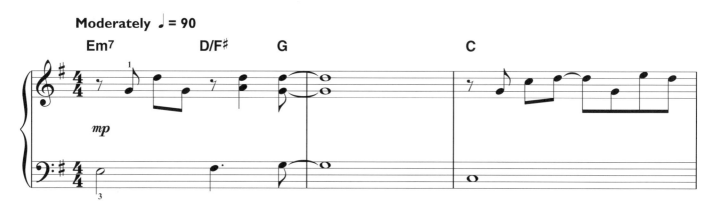

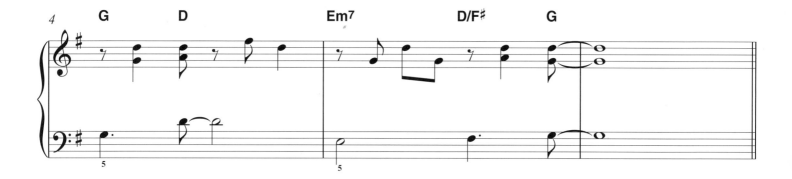

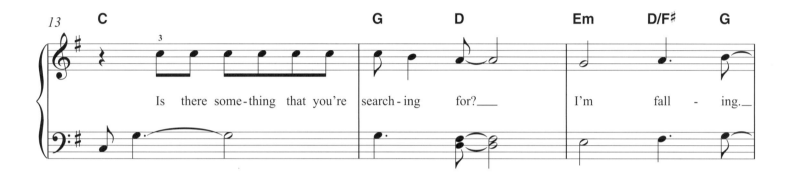

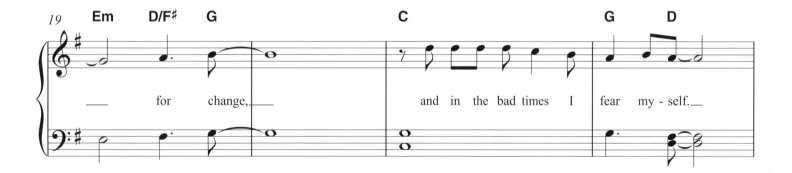

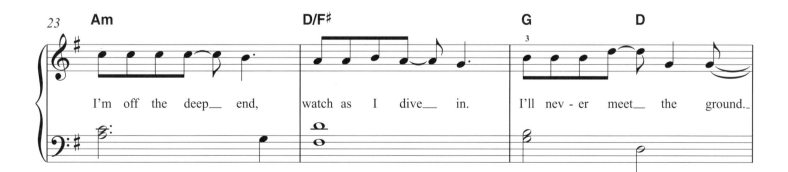

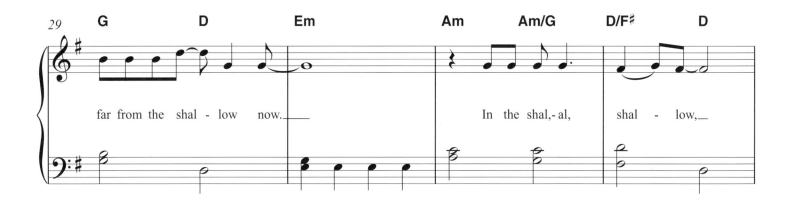

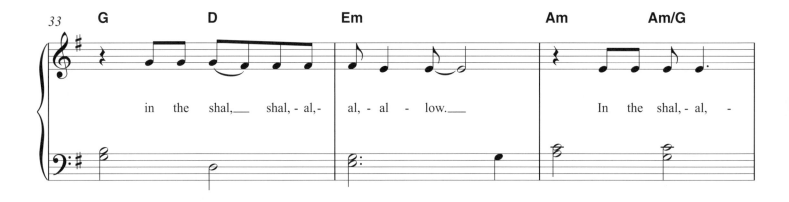

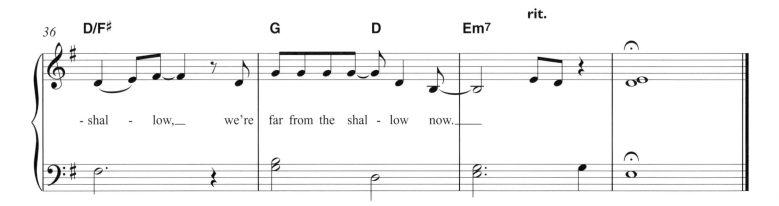

Trip a Little Light Fantastic
from Mary Poppins Returns

Music by Marc Shaiman
Lyrics by Scott Wittman and Marc Shaiman

Emily Blunt takes on the role of the beloved magic nanny, Mary Poppins, in this sequel to the original 1964 film.
As Bert (played by Dick Van Dyke) was Mary's sidekick in the first version, she is joined by Jack in *Mary Poppins Returns*,
played by Lin-Manuel Miranda, who sings this upbeat number in the film. For Emily Blunt, this was a nerve-wracking
role to take on, as Julie Andrews' version is so iconic, but she can rest assured — Andrews wrote
to the crew of *Mary Poppins Returns* and told them how much she loved it!

Hints & Tips: There should be a real sense of space at the beginning of this song; notice all the left-hand rests.
The music gradually increases in intensity and dynamic.

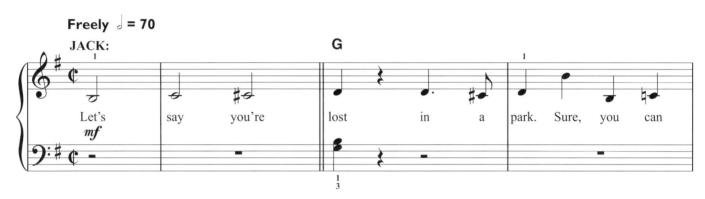

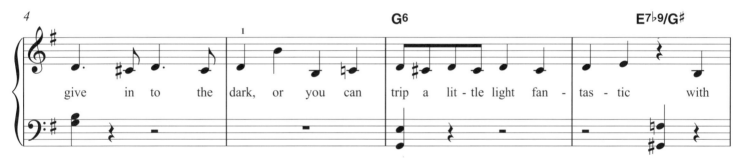

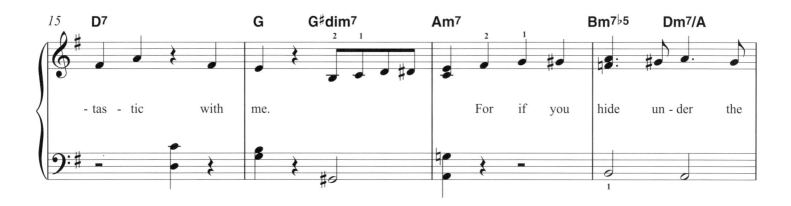

-tas - tic with me. For if you hide un - der the

cov - ers you might nev - er see the day but if a spark can start in -

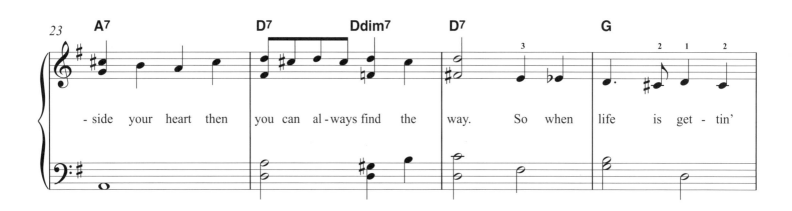

- side your heart then you can al - ways find the way. So when life is get - tin'

drea - ry, just pre - tend that you're a leer - ie as you trip a lit - tle light fan -

Faster

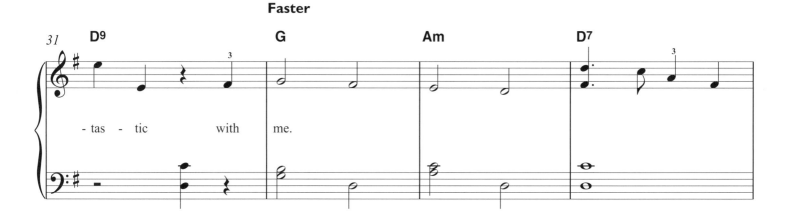

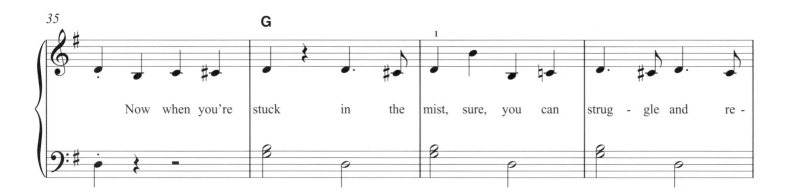

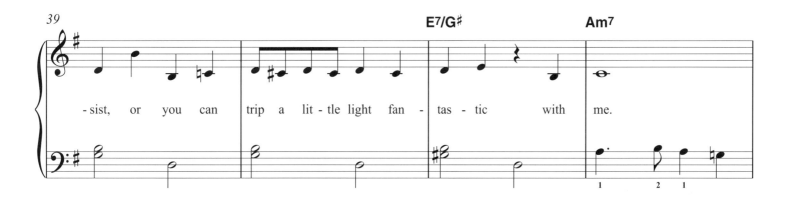

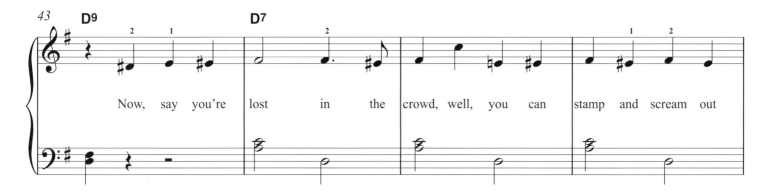

loud, or you can trip a lit-tle light fan - tas - tic with me.

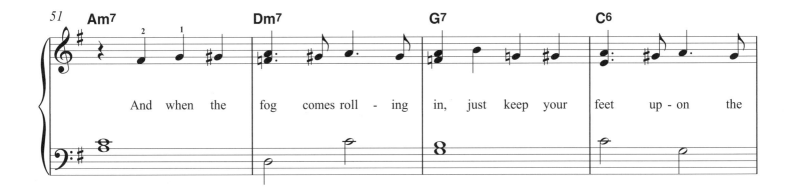

And when the fog comes roll - ing in, just keep your feet up - on the

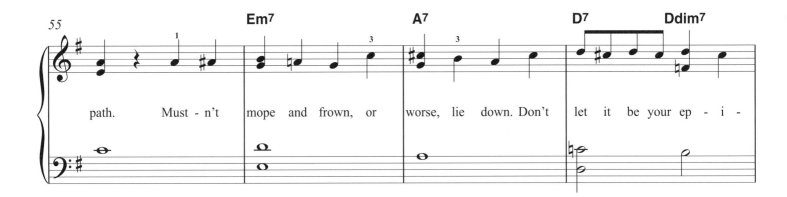

path. Must - n't mope and frown, or worse, lie down. Don't let it be your ep - i -

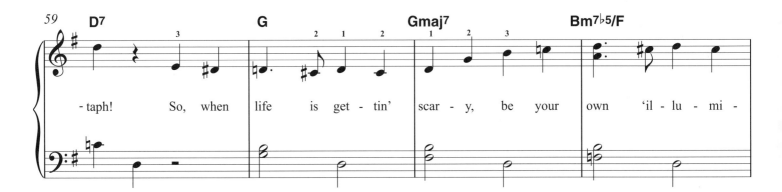

- taph! So, when life is get - tin' scar - y, be your own 'il - lu - mi -

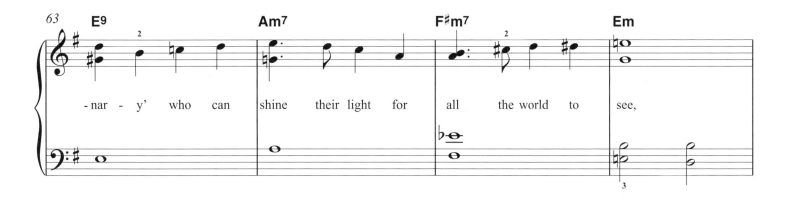

-nar - y' who can shine their light for all the world to see,

as you trip a lit - tle light fan - tas - tic. Won't you

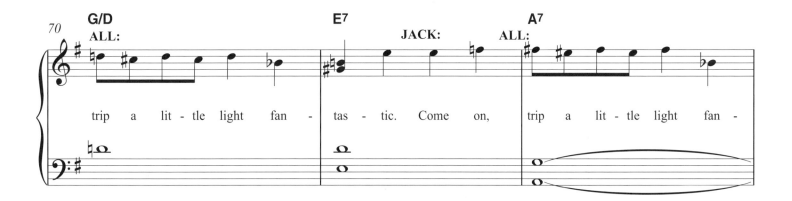

trip a lit - tle light fan - tas - tic. Come on, trip a lit - tle light fan -

-tas - tic with me!

This Is Me
from The Greatest Showman

Words and Music by Benj Pasek and Justin Paul

This smash hit from the 2017 film, *The Greatest Showman*, is sung by Keala Settle, who plays bearded woman, Lettie Lutz, in the movie. 'This Is Me' was written by Benj Pasek and Justin Paul and speaks about self-acceptance in the face of oppression, becoming the anthem of a film that celebrates the diversity of people. The powerful song won the Golden Globe for Best Original Song in 2018.

Hints & Tips: Make sure you are familiar with the key signature; there are a few places in the right hand where the C♯ could catch you off guard.

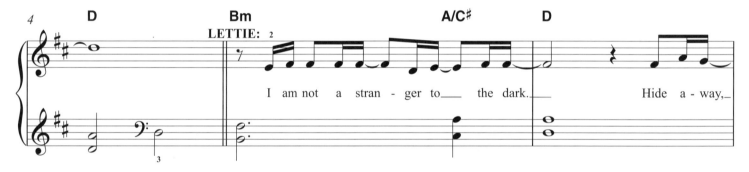

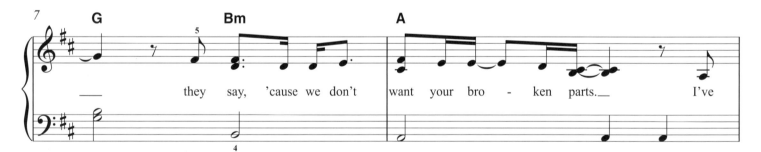

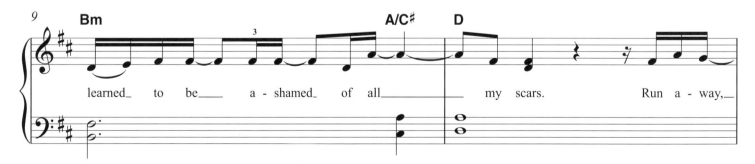

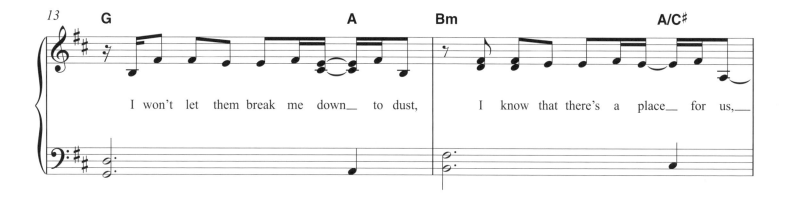

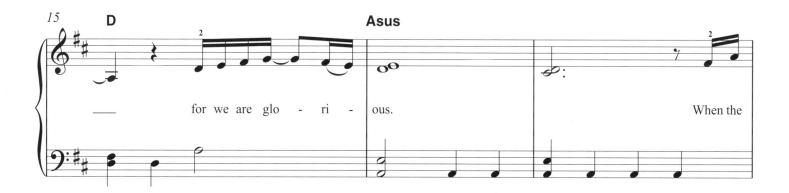

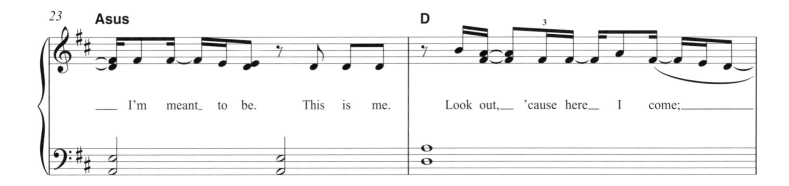

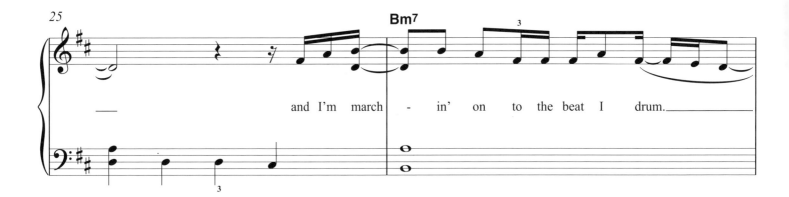

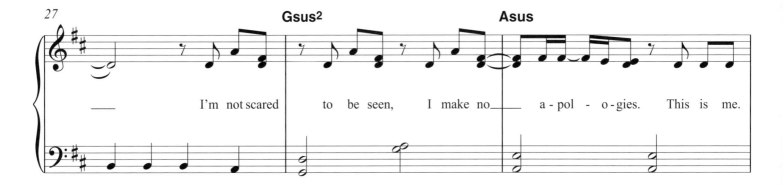

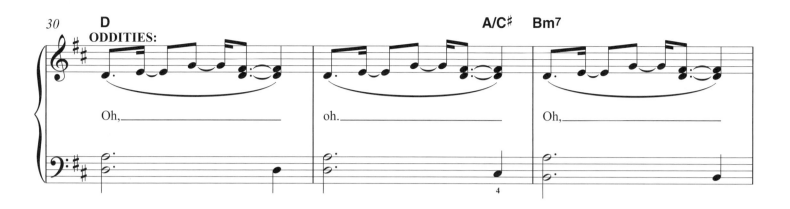

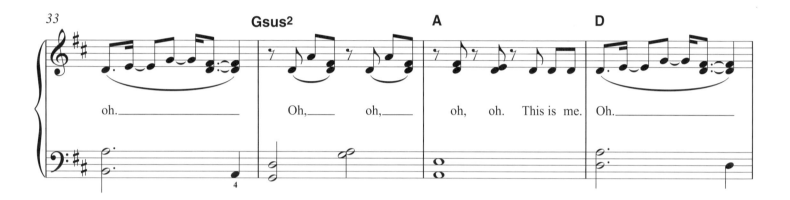

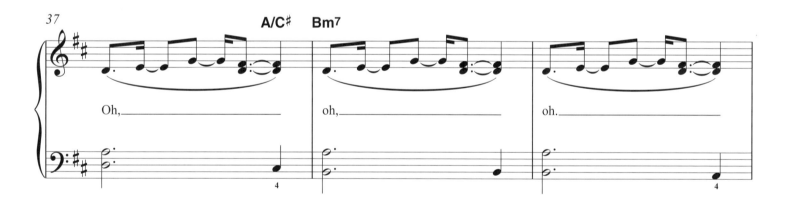

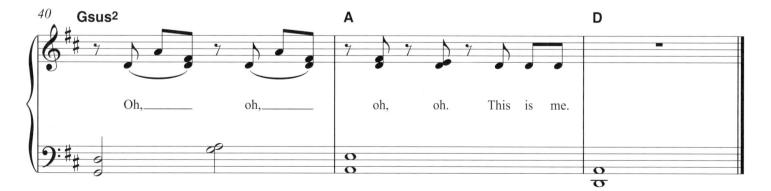

Discover our range of really easy piano bumper books...

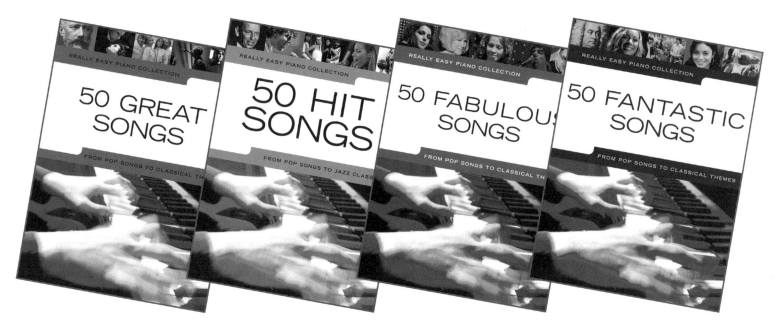

ORDER NO. AM995643   ORDER NO. AM1000615   ORDER NO. AM999449   ORDER NO. AM997744

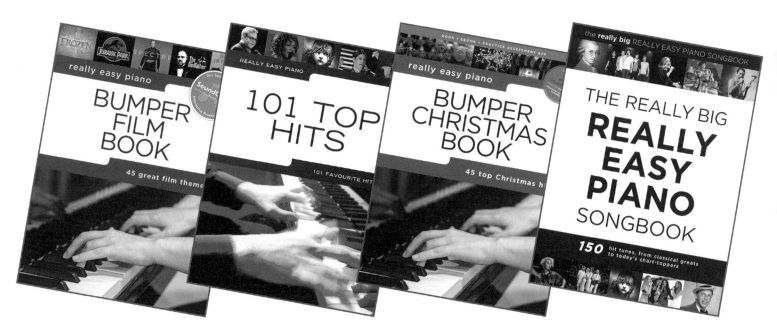

ORDER NO. HLE90004915   ORDER NO. AM1008975   ORDER NO. AM1013331   ORDER NO. AM1011032

Just visit your local music shop and ask
to see our huge range of music in print.